Pebble® Plus

Snakes

Anacondas

by Melissa Higgins

Consultants:
Christopher E. Smith, M.Sc., A.W.B.
President, Minnesota Herpetological Society
Gail Saunders-Smith, PhD,
consulting editor

CAPSTONE PRESS
a capstone imprint

Pebble Plus is published by Capstone Press,
1710 Roe Crest Drive, North Mankato, Minnesota 56003.
www.capstonepub.com

Library of Congress Cataloging-in-Publication Data
Higgins, Melissa, 1953–
Anacondas / by Melissa Higgins.
p. cm.—(Pebble plus. Snakes)
Summary: "Simple text and full-color photographs describe anacondas"—Provided by publisher.
Audience: 005-008.
Audience: K to grade 3.
Includes bibliographical references and index.
ISBN 978-1-4765-2066-7 (library binding)
ISBN 978-1-4765-3481-7 (eBook PDF)
1. Anaconda—Juvenile literature. I. Title.
QL666.O63H54 2014
597.96'7—dc23   2013007426

Editorial Credits
Jeni Wittrock, editor; Kyle Grenz, designer; Eric Manske, production specialist

Photo Credits
Alamy: blickwinkel/Schmidbauer, 9; Getty Images: age fotostock/Berndt Fischer, 19; National Geographic Stock: Ed George, 11; photoshot holdings: NHPA/Tony Crocetta, 7, Tom Brakefield, 13; Science Source: Francois Gohier, 17; Shutterstock: Dr. Morley Read, 5, Moneca, design element (throughout), Vadim Petrakov, 1; Super Stock Inc.: Juniors, cover, Minden Pictures, 15, NHPA, 21

Note to Parents and Teachers

The Snakes set supports national science standards related to biology and life science. This book describes and illustrates green anacondas. The images support early readers in understanding the text. The repetition of words and phrases helps early readers learn new words. This book also introduces early readers to subject-specific vocabulary words, which are defined in the Glossary section. Early readers may need assistance to read some words and to use the Table of Contents, Glossary, Read More, Internet Sites, and Index sections of the book.

Printed in the United States of America in North Mankato, Minnesota.
032013   007223CGF13.

Table of Contents

A Slithering Giant

A long, thick snake slips
quietly into a marsh.
It is a green anaconda, the
heaviest snake in the world.

Green anacondas grow
up to 25 feet (7.6 meters) long.
They can weigh more than
400 pounds (181 kilograms).

Watery Home

Green anacondas live in
South American swamps
and marshes. These reptiles are
hard to spot. Only their heads
peek above the water.

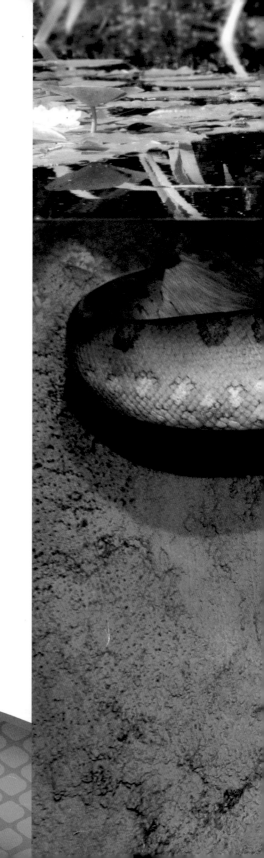

As good swimmers,

green anacondas glide

easily through water.

Riverbanks and branches

make sunny spots to rest.

Anaconda Range

☐ where anacondas live

North
America

Europe

Asia

Africa

N
W · E
S

South
America

Australia

Antarctica

Squeeze!

Green anacondas wait
for fish, turtles, and
deer to wander by.
Snatch! They grab their
prey with sharp teeth.

Green anacondas wrap
their bodies around prey.
They squeeze until the
prey stops breathing.

Open wide! The green anaconda swallows its meal in one bite. It may be months before this anaconda needs to eat again.

Family Life

Female anacondas give birth to 20 to 40 baby snakes. The babies are about 2 feet (61 centimeters) long.

Green anacondas can live
on their own when they
are born. They will live about
10 years in their watery homes.

Glossary

marsh—an area of soft wet land usually overgrown by grasses and low plants

prey—an animal that is hunted by another animal for food

reptile—a cold-blooded animal that breathes air and has a backbone; most reptiles have scales

riverbank—land next to a river

snatch—to grab

swamp—wet, spongy land often partly covered by water

Read More

Burke, Johanna. *Anaconda.* Killer Snakes. New York: Gareth Stevens Pub., 2011.

Ganeri, Anita. *Anaconda.* A Day in the Life: Rain Forest Animals. Chicago: Heinemann Library, 2011.

Gillenwater, Chadwick. *Anacondas.* South American Animals. North Mankato, Minn.: Capstone Press, 2012.

Internet Sites

FactHound offers a safe, fun way to find Internet sites related to this book. All of the sites on FactHound have been researched by our staff.

Here's all you do:

Visit *www.facthound.com*

Type in this code: 9781476520667

Super-cool stuff!

Check out projects, games and lots more at
www.capstonekids.com

Index

Word Count: 173
Grade: 1
Early-Intervention Level: 17